JULES FEIFFER

contributed his first strip to the *Village Voice* some eight years ago, and in the intervening time he has earned world fame as the brilliant satirist of a neurotic society. Today his work appears in more than forty newspapers, *Playboy* magazine, *The New Republic*, the Paris *Herald Tribune* and the London *Observer*. His books have been translated into six languages.

Mr. Feiffer has also illustrated a children's book, and his short cartoon film, *Munro*, based on the story in this book, won the Academy Award. His first novel, *Harry the Rat with Women*, appeared in 1963; and his one-act play, *Crawling Arnold*, had its premiere at Gian Carlo Menotti's Festival of Two Worlds at Spoleto.

Mr. Feiffer's *Sick, Sick, Sick; Boy, Girl. Boy, Girl; Hold Me!;* and *The Explainers* are published in Signet editions.

JULES FEIFFER

Passionella

AND OTHER STORIES

A SIGNET BOOK

Published by The New American Library

Published as a SIGNET BOOK
by arrangement with McGraw-Hill Book Company, Inc.

FIRST PRINTING, NOVEMBER, 1964

The story "Passionella" first appeared in *Pageant*, but was completely revised and redrawn for the McGraw-Hill edition. The story "Boom" first appeared in the *Village Voice*.

SIGNET TRADEMARK REG. U.S. PAT. OFF. AND FOREIGN COUNTRIES
REGISTERED TRADEMARK — MARCA REGISTRADA
HECHO EN CHICAGO, U.S.A.

SIGNET BOOKS are published by
The New American Library of World Literature, Inc.
501 Madison Avenue, New York, New York 10022

PRINTED IN THE UNITED STATES OF AMERICA

A
word
from
John Crosby

"Passionella," the title story of this slim, neurotic volume, is about a chimney sweep who, with the assistance of her "friendly neighborhood godmother," becomes a big-bosomed movie star. Well, sure it sounds like Cinderella, but it's as geared to our generation as George Bernard Shaw's version of Cinderella (which he called "Pygmalion") was geared to his.

Passionella's Prince Charming, for example, snaps his fingers, wears a black leather jacket, and says things like, "Do you dig Beckett, man?" Passionella's coach turns to a pumpkin not at midnight, but at the precise moment the Late, Late Show goes off the air, a time of night more in tune with our restless generation than midnight. Feiffer is a wick-edly witty observer of our time and our screwy problems, but even more of our screwy rationalizations. One of these essays is about a man who is the lone occupant of the moon. Watching this guy think himself from one mental block to another — first praying for rescue from the moon and finally, when it comes, prepared to repel invaders — is a delicious study in contemporary behavior.

This book is a splendid successor to *Sick, Sick, Sick*, Feiffer's notable guide to non-confident living, but it's a little different in scope and aim. The stories in this one—there are four — are quite a lot longer, the characters a little deeper, and the techniques a little more sure-footed. For such a funny fellow, Feiffer is essentially a serious humorist—an appellation I hope won't cost him sales — and the final essay in the book on the Bomb is frightening, though funny. Feiffer, in short, is trying to make us think as well as laugh, and I guarantee that last story will stick to your ribs quite a spell.

Each cartoonist has his own distinctive line, his own point of departure from the human race — if he hasn't, he'd better turn in his pencil—and Feiffer's slant on things seems closer to events than, say, that of James Thurber or Walt Kelly, two other talented pencil-pushers.

The reason for this is simply that Feiffer *is* closer to events. He's only thirty years old. That means he's younger than Mauldin and almost younger than anyone. His characters—his wistfully droopy girls and his shaggy, introspective men—have an authentic flavor of *right now* about them. They don't have the Depression or Hitler on the horizon, as did my generation. Apart from the Bomb, their miseries are rather shadowy ones; but this, if anything, makes them even more miserable, since it gives them more time to worry about their own personal inadequacies.

For this reason, I'm tempted to call Feiffer the *minnesinger* of the Beat Generation, whose woes he draws with charm and a gentle, fragile humor. "Most people I've met talk too easily about problems that a generation ago would have made people commit suicide," he has said. "People can become so blasé about their emotional miseries that relating symptoms can become an important part of social life. I wouldn't dare offer a solution. I just do cartoons that point the problem out."

To my mind, Feiffer is the first to point out this curious contemporary madness. I have the feeling that his cartoon characters are more isolated than anyone else's, more wrapped in their private worlds, each striving to communicate to a monstrously indifferent outside world and having a terrible time of it. Like Munro. Here's a four-year-old kid who gets drafted into the Army and no one will pay attention to him until he bursts into tears. That's the history of the world, really.

Passionella

ELLA

was a chimneysweep.

She worked in a big office building downtown.

But it wasn't what she really wanted to do. As she often tried to tell people:

I'M ONLY DOING THIS TO MAKE A LIVING

Every night after work Ella would go home to her lonely furnished room, and there she'd sit, all night, in front of the TV and think but one thought:

IF I
COULD
ONLY
BE A
BEAUTIFUL
GLAMOROUS.
MOVIE
STAR

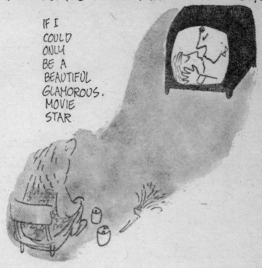

And that was how she spent her days —

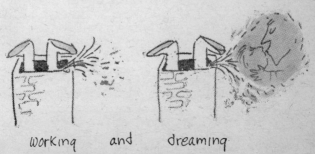

working   and   dreaming

Then one day Ella's employer came to her chimney and said: ELLA
WE
WON'T
NEED
YOU
AFTER
NEXT
WEEK.
AUTOMATION
HAS
COME
TO
CHIMNEY
SWEEPING!

Ella was unemployed!

For weeks she wandered the streets looking for work. But nowhere was a good old-fashioned craftswoman needed.

She began to go hungry.

Television was her only escape. From the time she arrived home till the time she fell asleep, her eyes never wandered from the screen.

SOMEDAY
I WILL
BE A
BEAUTIFUL
GLAMOROUS
MOVIE
STAR.

Then one evening (it was the night of the full moon).
Ella returned from a thankless day of job hunting,
turned on the set and ...there was no picture!

She stood before the TV stunned, disbelieving, her
eyes searched the screen for the trace of an image.

NO PICTURE

NO PICTURE

NO PICTURE

Then Ella heard a voice:

HELLO OUT THERE!
THIS IS YOUR
FRIENDLY
NEIGHBORHOOD
GODMOTHER
COME TO
BRING YOU
THE ANSWER
TO YOUR
MOST
CHERISHED
DREAMS!

YOU ARE NOW ALL YOU
EVER WANTED TO BE.
HENCEFORTH YOU SHALL
BE KNOWN AS
PASSIONELLA!
THIS IS YOUR FRIENDLY
NEIGHBORHOOD
GODMOTHER RETURNING
YOU TO YOUR
LOCAL NETWORK.

Ella could not believe her eyes. She was dazzling.
"NOW I SHALL BECOME A BEAUTIFUL, GLAMOROUS MOVIE STAR!"
she said and she ran off to El Morocco—

where she met Ed Sullivan, Walter Winchell, Earl
Wilson and Cholly Knickerbocker—all of whom promised to do columns on her. And this also happened:

"I AM A FAMOUS MOTION PICTURE
PRODUCER, COME TO THE
STUDIO TOMORROW MORNING
AND I WILL SIGN YOU TO A
LIFE TIME
CONTRACT."

Passionella went home bursting with joy. The next morning, without bothering to look in the mirror, she rushed off to the movie studio.

LIFETIME
CONTRACT?
ARE YOU
OUT OF
YOUR
HEAD?

There she was -   her homely old self.

Then it was all just a dream!

Ella walked the streets till the sun set. 'IM NOT ASKING MUCH' she brooded. ITS NOT AS IF I WANT TO BE A **RICH** BEAUTIFUL GLAMOROUS MOVIE STAR— OR EVEN A **WELL LIKED** BEAUTIFUL GLAMOROUS MOVIE STAR. I JUST WANT TO BE A BEAUTIFUL GLAMOROUS MOVIE STAR FOR ITS **OWN** SAKE

Then as the moon lit the sky she returned home.

THIS IS
YOUR
FRIENDLY
NEIGHBORHOOD
GODMOTHER
WHERE
YOU
BEEN?

"LOOK AT ME!" cried Ella "I'M JUST THE WAY
I'VE ALWAYS BEEN!"
"ARE YOU INDEED?" snickered the TV set
and suddenly —

YOUR FRIENDLY NEIGHBORHOOD
GODMOTHER ONLY HAS POWER
FROM "HUNTLEY-BRINKLEY"
TO THE "LATE LATE SHOW."
DURING THOSE HOURS YOU
SHALL BE RAVISHING. YOU
SHALL BE PASSIONELLA!

A-AND THE
REST OF
THE DAY

THE REST OF
THE DAY, MY
DEAR, YOU
ARE ON
SUSTAINING.

And with that her friendly neighborhood
godmother signed off.

in the months
that followed
a new star
was born:
the mysterious
exotic
bewitching
temptress...

Passionella

Prevue
PASSIONELLA
in
the SINNER

A legend grew around her. Strange stories circulated.
Stories of how she would only allow her films to be
shot between the hours of 'Huntley-Brinkley'
and the 'Late Late Show' and how at 3 a.m. she
would hop into her sports car and vanish.

"WHO IS THIS MYSTERIOUS PASSIONELLA?" fans and
columnists wondered. "WHAT IS HER SECRET?"
asked show business.

And as her mystery grew, so did her popularity. Her pictures set new attendance records.

Songs were written about her.

She was in demand everywhere. And when there were no pictures to make, life became a ceaseless round of cocktail parties, night-club parties, publicity parties, beat parties.

But was Passionella happy?' Now that she had money,
fame, glamor, excitement - was she truly content?
Let us hear the answer
in her own words:
"I
AM
NOT
TRULY
CONTENT"

She began to feel
a vague discomfort -

A certain
indefinable
unhappiness

"DON'T FEEL UNHAPPY" said her producers

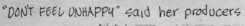

and they bought her a new house.

"DON'T FEEL UNHAPPY" said
her directors –

and they bought her a swimming pool for her new house.

"DON'T FEEL UNHAPPY" said her legion of
faithful fans –

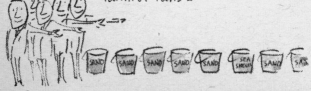

And they bought her a beach to go with the
swimming pool of her new house.

But Passionella was still not happy...

WHAT DOES
IT ALL MEAN
IF I CAN
NOT HAVE
LOVE?

She spent her nights acting and her days weeping.

OH HOW
HOLLOW
IS ALL THIS
BEAUTY
WITHOUT
THE RIGHT
MAN TO
SHARE
IT
WITH.

Finally she spoke to her friendly neighborhood godmother

MY FIELD IS STRICTLY PUBLIC RELATIONS. YOU'LL HAVE TO HANDLE YOUR OWN EMOTIONAL PROBLEMS.

And then one day Passionella met the right man...

CRAZY

her
new
co-star-
the
idol
of
a
million
teenagers.
FLIP
(THE PRINCE)
CHARMING!

snap
snap
snap

The Prince represented the youth
movement in Hollywood

He hated cops.

He hated reporters.

He hated movies.

Passionella had never met such a man.

Glamor did not interest him.

Making love did not interest him.

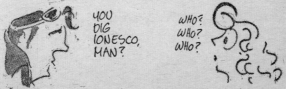

Only spiritual things interested him...

Passionella left him cold. He had but one passion.
ACTING, MAN, ACTING!
THE CHICK WHO MAKES
THIS CAT SWING HAS
GOT TO E·MOTE, MAN·
E·MOTE!

Act! In all her years as a movie star no one
had wanted Passionella to act
"HOW DOES
ONE GO
ABOUT IT?"she asked
her beloved.

"MAN·"
he replied.
"GO
TO
SCHOOL."

And she did

THE
INNER
ME
ACTING
ACADEMY

Now, the 'Inner Me Acting Academy' was where all the movie stars went to learn how to act. It could take young, pretty, dimple cheeked starlets -

And after months of study teach them how to act like:

confused juvenile delinquents - disillusioned drug addicts - sensitive gun fighters - misunderstood Nazis

"SO THAT'S WHAT
ACTING IS" mused
          Passionella

"YES" said the
school master.
"WE ARE LEARN-
ING TO PORTRAY
THE REAL PEOPLE."

The next day Passionella went to the head of her studio.

"I AM TIRED OF BEING A CARDBOARD FIGURE ON A TINSEL BACKGROUND." she said

"OH" said the studio head

So there it was. And there was nothing anybody could do about it. "IF I CAN NOT PLAY A CHIMNEY SWEEP I SHALL RETIRE FROM THE SCREEN."

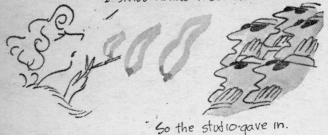

"So the studio gave in."

GLAMOR GIRL TO PORTRAY CHIMNEY SWEEP

cried the newspapers.

LIFE

Can she really act?

asked the magazines.

TIME

amid the cinders a busty rose?

And the world waited to find out.

"The Chimney Sweep" was budgeted as a twenty million dollar production.

NEVER BEFORE SUCH TURGID REALISM!

WE WILL EVEN SHOOT IT IN THE BRONX!

drummed the press agents

proclaimed the publicists.

No expense was spared. The very best black listed screen writers were flown in from England to do the scenario.

Then came word that Passionella had consented to a **daytime** shooting schedule. A nation of 175 million reeled back, stunned. Passionella went on "Youth Wants To Know."

"YES, IRWIN. FROM NOW ON I WILL PERFORM **ONLY** DURING THE DAY."

In the weeks that followed the eyes of six continents fastened on a secluded mansion in Beverly Hills.

And then came the first day of shooting. Half a state gathered to see the **new** Passionella leave for the studio.

"MARVELOUS!" cried the
producer.
"UNBELIEVABLE!" cried the
director.
"I THINK SHE'S OVERACTING."
muttered a
jealous star
from a rival studio.

WE WILL USE
NO DOUBLES!
announced the studio.

PASSIONELLA WILL
SWEEP ALL HER
OWN CHIMNEYS!

No one could remember a screen personality ever fitting a role so perfectly.

But every day promptly at six, as the sun began to go down, Passionella would hop into her sports car and vanish.

Finally the picture was completed. 'The Chimney Sweep' was previewed at a special showing for landlords.

It drew raves.

"AT LAST MOVIES HAVE COME OF AGE" said the Saturday Review

"PASSIONELLA IS A CINCH TO COP THE OSCAR" said Hedda, Louella, Sidney, Sheila, Hy and Cholly Knickerbocker.

The award was presented by last years winner, FLIP (the Prince) CHARMING — who whispered:

Their engagement was announced on the spot

Dreamy eyed, the two lovers went home where they passed the night making tender love.

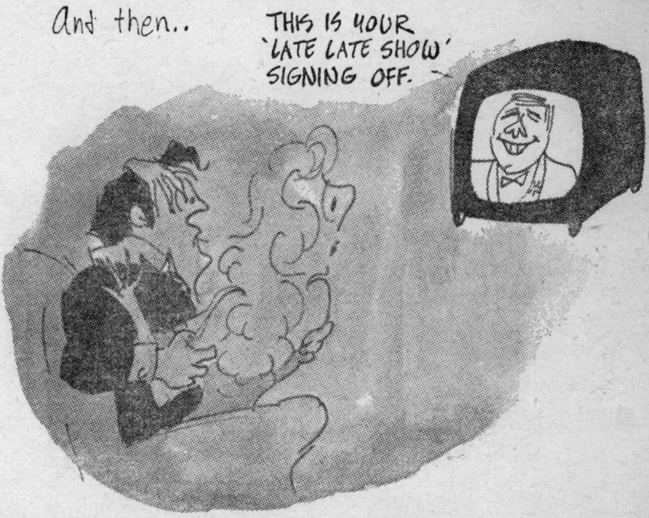
And then..
THIS IS YOUR 'LATE LATE SHOW' SIGNING OFF.

It was three a.m. The two lovers stared at each other aghast

And they lived happily ever after.

Munro

Now
this
is
all
about
Munro

who was four

There was nothing unusual about Munro.

He wouldn't eat.   *NO!*

He wouldn't sleep   *NO!*

He hated little girls.   *GRRR!*

His was a stable, well rounded, fully integrated life.

Then one day he received a letter...

He had one of his big friends read it to him.

IT'S FROM LOCAL
DRAFT BOARD 9-Z
AND IT SAYS
YOUR FRIENDS
AND NEIGHBORS
SEND YOU
GREETINGS.

So while other children jumped rope and hula hooped and chased each other around the block, and did exactly what it was normal for them to do, Munro came to the shocking realization that at the age of four, **he** had been drafted.

The next morning without telling his mother (she always took on so). Munro went for his physical

UNBUTTON
ME,
MISTER.

He took a whole series of tests. He took an intelligence test.

and a height test...

HEIGHT: SIX FOOT TWO!

All along Munro tried to explain that he was just a little boy - but the doctors were too busy drafting a famous singer to ever even notice him.

And so Munro was classified 1A.

BUTTON
ME,
MISTER.

GO HOME AND SETTLE ALL YOUR BUSINESS AFFAIRS. YOU'LL HEAR FROM US IN TWENTY-ONE DAYS.

Of course, Munro didn't say anything for fear someone might call him unpatriotic. He went on home and didn't tell a soul. (His mother always took on so.)

In twenty one days a second letter came. This one was from the **President** himself, which made Munro feel better about the whole thing.

So with a bar of soap, some chocolate cigarettes and a toothbrush Munro went to war

TEN'HOOT

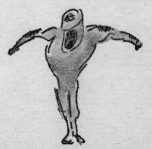

The Sergeant couldn't speak English very well.

FOOR'RIT HOO

He spoke in code

HUP
HOOP
HIP
HO
HUP
HOO
HIP
HO

Munro thought he was crazy.

First thing, Munro and all the others were marched off to a big hall to hear an important looking man talk. The man explained they were all there because of a world struggle. It seemed that one side was in favor of God and the other was not. The man used very simple words. Even Munro could understand.

When the man was finished, everyone was marched off again.

Now Munro was a full fledged soldier.

He learned to play
all the games
that soldiers play.
like "FACE"...

RI' FACE
LEF' FACE
UP FACE
DOWN FACE
IN FACE
OUT FACE
FACE FACE

Or another game called "TAKE THIS MAN'S NAME" where everyone must sweep and clean to make the barracks as shiny as they could ever be and then the man who was "IT" would walk past each bunk with a cranky look on his face and say: TAKE THIS MAN'S NAME!
TAKE THIS MAN'S NAME!
TAKE...

Or another game called "BENDOVER" where if you are "IT," you had to go to the Kitchen and bendover while you

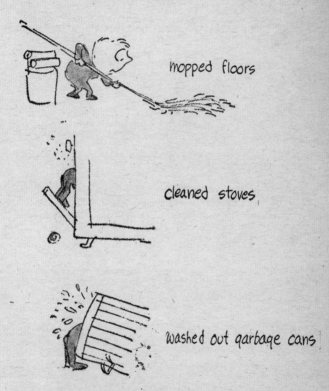

mopped floors

cleaned stoves

washed out garbage cans

Oh, there were so many games to play. Just when Munro would think they were all out along came a new one.

After awhile he grew tired of playing.
He lost all his zest for

mud

guns

food

But the sergeants

And the captains

And the
colonels

And
the
generals -

always loved to play. They never seemed to get tired.

But poor Munro was very tired. So he went to the sergeant and he said:

The sergeant did not look up. Sergeants are very busy people.

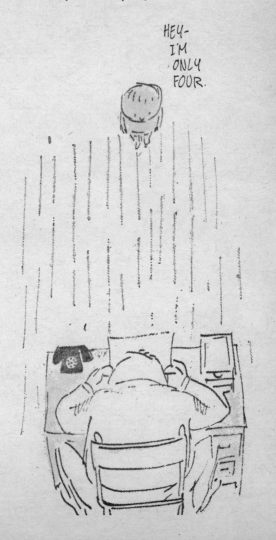

The sergeant still did not look up The way to always tell its a sergeant is if he doesn't ever look up. Finally he said

IT IS THE OFFICIAL POLICY OF THE ARMY NOT TO DRAFT MEN OF FOUR. ERGO YOU CANNOT BE FOUR. ERGO YOU ONLY **THINK** YOU ARE FOUR. GO ON. SICK CALL

So the next morning Munro went on sick call

Sick call was held in a big crowded room. Some times it was drafty Sometimes it was over heated. "KEEPS THEM ON THEIR TOES" reasoned the policy makers. Every once in a while a doctor would walk through the room, muttering in a low voice...

Finally it was Munro's turn

Munro was sent on his way with a box of white pills
and a warning to stop faking. Sick call was over.

But try as he might, Munro just could not get over the idea that he was four. He went to the psychiatrist.

analyzed the psychiatrist.

He went to the chaplain.

MY SON, YOU WILL FIND
LIFE HERE IN THE ARMY
SO MUCH MORE REWARD-
ING IF YOU MAKE THE
BEST OF IT AND DECIDE
TO FACE REALITIES. LETS
HAVE ANOTHER CHAT
REAL SOON.

...quoth the chaplain.

He went to a colonel

GET OUTTA HERE Y'LITTLE GOOFUP OR I'LL SHOVE YA IN THE STOCKADE FOR A MONTH!

... opined the colonel.

He went before a whole board of captains and majors and colonels who had all once been social workers on the lower east side so that they understood about people. They stared at Munro a long time. Then they said:

GO BACK AND TRY!

Munro promised he would try — really try this time For if so many wise men claimed it was impossible for him to be four, how indeed could he be?

So Munro returned to the barracks, his little
back aching, his little legs weary. This was
to be his life from now on.

He would march with the best of them

He would shoot with the best of them.

And, if need be, he would go to war
with the best of them.

And as he walked he saw a new bunch of men - all marching along out of step - all looking very unhappy.

Munro just stood there and watched.

"SEE THAT MAN!" said the sergeant suddenly pointing at Munro. All the new men looked.

"THAT'S A **SOLDIER!**" said the sergeant proudly. "THAT'S WHAT WE'RE GOING TO TRAIN **YOU** TO BE!"

All the men looked

"WE'RE GOING TO
SEPARATE THE
MEN FROM THE
BOYS!" said
the sergeant

And Munro began to cry.

Right there in the middle of the field, he cried and cried.

"STOP THAT CRYING, SOLDIER!" said the sergeant and he looked embarrassed.

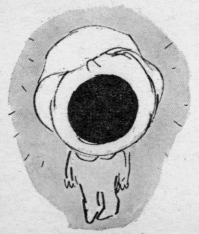

Munro cried louder.

"STOP THAT CRYING, SOLDIER!" said the colonel and he came running out of his office looking very upset.

Munro only cried louder

Out ran the doctor.

Out ran the psychiatrist.

Out ran the chaplain.

No one had heard such a sound in the middle of an army camp before.

"STOP! YOU **MUST** STOP THAT CRYING, SOLDIER!"
they all said.

But Munro wouldn't.

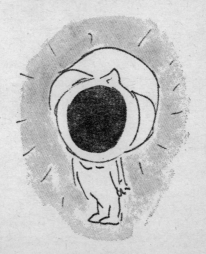

Then out came the general.

Everyone stepped back. Everyone saluted.

Except Munro – who cried.

"SOLDIERS DON'T CRY" said the general.
Everyone nodded

Munro cried.

"ONLY LITTLE BOYS CRY." said the general.
Everyone nodded.

Munro cried.

"ARE YOU A SOLDIER OR A LITTLE TEENSY WEENSY HELPLESS CRYING BABY BOY?" demanded the general.
"YEAH!" said everybody.

Munro just cried.

The general stared at him scornfully.
"OBVIOUSLY THEN YOU'RE NOTHING BUT A
LITTLE BABY BOY!"

"OBVIOUSLY" said the colonel scornfully.

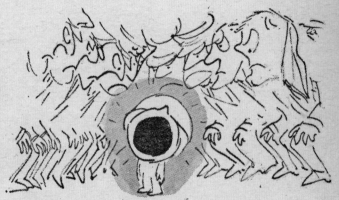

"OBVIOUSLY," said the doctor, the chaplain, the psychiatrist, the whole board of captains and majors and colonels scornfully.

"OBVIOUSLY" said the new bunch of men.

And suddenly—once they had said it—
Monro looked different to them.

He looked like a little boy!

The general blinked his eyes
and stared very hard.

He stared harder than he'd ever
stared in his whole life.

And then finally he said:

I RULE
THAT **THIS**
IS A
LITTLE
BOY.

Everyone nodded in agreement. "WHO COULD EVER
THINK THIS WAS ANYTHING BUT A LITTLE BOY," they
said And they made out it was all a big joke.

They pinched Munro's cheeks.

They tousled his hair.

They gave him a release to sign.

The day Munro was sent home they held a big parade in his honor.

There were newsreel photographers and live television and his mother and his father and all the kids in the neighborhood and even another message from the President—

"I HOLD NO FEAR FOR OUR NATION'S FUTURE WHEN EVEN A MERE LAD OF FOUR IS STIRRED STRONGLY ENOUGH BY OUR CAUSE TO ENLIST HIMSELF IN THE SERVICE OF HIS COUNTRY."

And a man from the American Legion came around asking him to join.

He was awarded a medal, a set of military brushes,
and a whole box of toy nuclear weapons
Munro was a hero!

Oh, his parents were **very** proud.

But from that time on, whenever he became cranky—

and wouldn't eat—

No!

and wouldn't sleep—

No!

and hated little girls—

...GRRR!

his mother would just remind him of the army—

and Munro would be a good boy –

a very good boy indeed.

George's
Moon

Once

there was a man named George –

who lived on the moon

no kidding.

George didn't have much to do on the moon.

He slept.

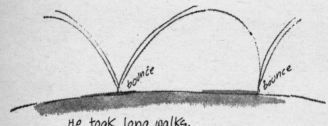

bounce   bounce

He took long walks.

He kept trying to figure
out how he got there.

THERE **MUST**
BE A
LOGICAL
EXPLANATION

But he never made any headway.

Aside from feeling that he was basically **non-moon**, he had no idea **who** he was or **how** he got there. All he knew definitely was that undoubtedly his name was George.

ONE **MUST** BEGIN SOMEWHERE.

And that somehow he was unique.

SOMETIMES
I FEEL
RATHER
SMUG
ABOUT
IT.

3.

HI THERE,
MY MOON.

4

5.

SOMEDAY
I'LL CHANGE
YOUR NAME
TO GEORGE.

6.

But this was a false exuberance. George felt no real connection with the land.

HOW CAN I WHEN I BOUNCE ALL THE TIME.

Mostly he was concerned with his **roots**. He thought about his roots quite a bit. But no matter how hard he thought he couldn't come up with a thing.

 — SIGH

So then he'd concentrate on his values. Because if he could sort out his values it would tell him something about his background and if he knew something about his background it would then give him some indication of his roots.

S/64

But he couldn't come up with a single value.

All of which was pretty depressing.

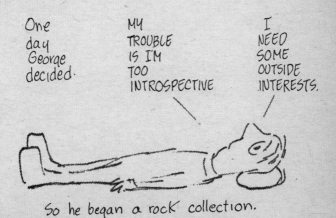

One day George decided.

MY TROUBLE IS I'M TOO INTROSPECTIVE

I NEED SOME OUTSIDE INTERESTS.

So he began a rock collection.

Rocks had no meaning for George. He began to count craters.

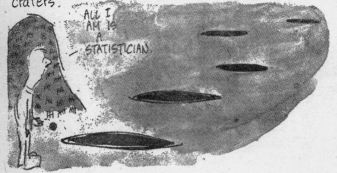

George felt he was thinking too much. He needed to regain the feeling of his body. So he learned to drop kick his rock collection into his craters.

500 POINTS.

But he ran out of rocks.

He was just filling up
time and he knew it.
What good was it to
collect rocks, to
count craters, to
fill the craters
you've counted
with the rocks
you've collected,
to empty the craters
and collect the
rocks all over
again?
Was this a way for a man to spend a life?

IT
LACKS
DIGNITY.

George recognized
he had no sense
of himself. Also that
he had no sense of
others. How could he
have any dignity
without a context?
He didn't know who
he was or what
or anything.

A MAN
HAS TO
BELIEVE
IN
SOMETHING.

So since **he** was the only thing around, George decided to believe in himself.

HAIL GEORGE.

He made up poems to himself.

GEORGE
George
GEORGE
george
GEORGE
George
GEORGE.

He made up stories to himself.

SO GEORGE CURED THE PLAGUE, ENDED THE FAMINE, TURNED BACK THE FLOOD.

And then he awoke one morning and found that he had forgotten his name.

THAT'S WHAT
I GET.
SERVES ME
RIGHT.

So he stopped believing in himself.

He looked around for something
else to believe in He tried to
believe in rocks.

HAIL.

But they seemed so ordinary.

He tried to believe in craters.

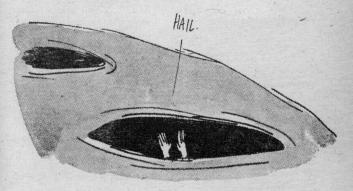

HAIL.

But since he had kicked rocks into them
he hadn't much respect for craters.

He made up other things to believe in. But they were all inadequate. He needed something spectacular. Something way beyond his experience. Then one day he looked up and noticed space.

There were all sorts of advantages to believing in space.
For one thing it was out there - **way** out there —
AND IT
FILLS UP
EVERYTHING.
THAT'S PRETTY
IMPRESSIVE

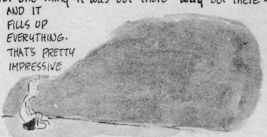

And it was obviously unknown.

IT COULD
NEVER BE
DISILLUSIONING

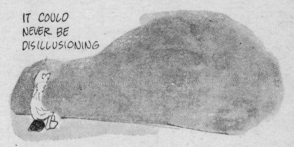

And it was dark with white blotches - very attractive
really - much more imposing than all those rocks
and craters he **used** to worship.

IT'S AMAZING
HOW I'VE
MATURED IN
MY BELIEFS.

George spent his days dreaming about space.

IF SPACE IS **REALLY** THERE AND I **KNOW** IT MUST BE THERE BECAUSE I CAN SEE IT.

THEN **I** MUST BE REALLY **HERE** OR ELSE I WOULDN'T KNOW ITS **THERE** BECAUSE I COULDN'T SEE IT.

AND IF I **AM** HERE AND **I** CAN SEE SPACE THEN SPACE MUST, IN ALL LOGIC, BE ABLE TO SEE **ME.**

—WHICH PROVES THAT I **EXIST.**

SPACE AND GEORGE— GEORGE AND SPACE —

A TEAM.

It almost made him feel like crying.

Then one day they started shooting rockets off at him.

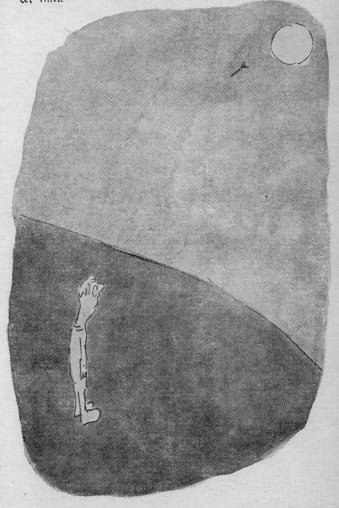

George was overjoyed.

THEY'RE COMING FOR ME!

THIS WAY FELLA'S, THIS WAY!

George tied a red undershirt to a big rock.

IF YOU **REALLY** BELIEVE, IT **HAS** TO COME TRUE.

But the rocket didn't even come close.

George wasn't too sad. Space was no longer mysterious and intangible. Space had people in it and they were trying to rescue him. He sat all day on the dark side and dreamed about them:

FIRST OF ALL THEY MUST BE VERY KIND TO GO TO ALL THIS TROUBLE. THEY MUST BE VERY HUMAN-ITARIAN AND HAVE LOTS OF FAVORITE CHARITIES.

THEY WILL COME HERE AND WE'LL HAVE A BIG PARTY AND I'LL BE VERY POLITE AND ASK THEM IF THEY'D LIKE TO STAY OVER BUT THEY'LL SAY - "WELL, WE **DO** HAVE TO GET BACK."

AND THEN WE'LL TAKE OFF AND I'LL BE **HOME** (WHEREVER THAT IS) AND THERE'LL BE BIG PARADES AND TESTIMONIAL DINNERS.

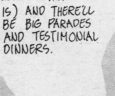

ALL BECAUSE **I'M** THE ONLY EXPERT ON THE MOON!

But then George realized he **wasn't** an expert on the moon. In fact he really didn't know much about it at all.

— I ONLY LIVE HERE.

He didn't know whether those holes actually **were** craters or not. Maybe they were coal mines.

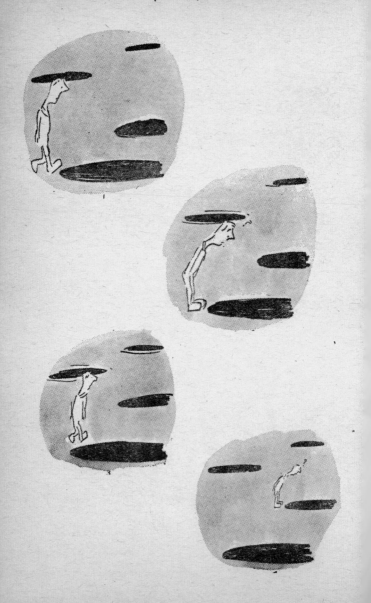

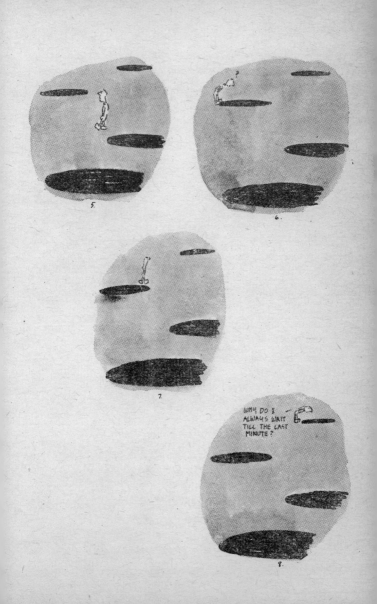

He didn't know why it was that he could bounce or how come he could breathe without a helmet or why he was never hungry though there wasn't any food to eat.

MY TROUBLE IS I'M NOT VERY OBSERV- ANT.

THEY'LL COME EXPECTING ALL KINDS OF INFORMA- TION AND WHAT CAN I TELL THEM?

NOTHING!

OH, I'M SURE THEY'LL BE VERY NICE ABOUT IT. THEY'LL PRETEND NOT EVEN TO NOTICE.

THEY'LL SAY- "MY, BUT DON'T YOU DRESS NEATLY."

I'LL FEEL LIKE A FOOL!

And then one day they shot off another rocket.

George hung up his undershirt again but on a less conspicuous rock. He began to feel anxious about the whole thing.

WHAT DO THEY WANT FROM ME? I'M NOT ANALYTICAL. THEY'LL JUST HAVE TO UNDERSTAND.

A FAT LOT **THEY'LL** CARE! THEY'LL BE **SCIENTISTS!** COLD- DISPASSIONATE- NO TIME FOR **MY** PROBLEMS.

THEY PROBABLY
DON'T EVEN
KNOW I'M
HERE!

But once more the rocket did not come close.

WISE
GUYS.

But George knew that ultimately they **would** come
He spent all his days sitting on the dark side
and dreaming about what it would be like.

THEY'LL COME OUT OF
THOSE DAMN ROCKETS
AND I BET FIRST
THING THEY'LL DO IS
STICK UP A **FLAG**

THEIR
FLAG
ON MY
MOON!

THEN THEY'LL
GIVE ME THEIR
BAGS TO CARRY.

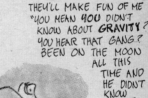

THEY'LL MAKE FUN OF ME
"YOU MEAN **YOU** DIDN'T
KNOW ABOUT **GRAVITY**?
YOU HEAR THAT GANG?
BEEN ON THE MOON
ALL THIS
TIME AND
HE DIDN'T
KNOW
ABOUT
GRAVITY!"

AND THEY'LL
TELL LOTS
OF INSIDE
JOKES.

"WELL WE'D **LOVE** TO TAKE
YOU BACK" THEY'LL SAY-
"BUT YOU SEE HOW
CROWDED WE ARE WITH
ALL THESE ROCK
SAMPLES. WOULD YOU
MIND GIVING US A
SHOVE?"

George thought about the way it used to be. The fun he had drop kicking rocks into craters. What a ball it was to sit around the moon and think about his roots.

THEY'VE SPOILED IT!

And then one day they shot off another rocket.

George used body english to make it go away.

But the rocket kept coming –

ITS AN INVASION!

Then, suddenly the fear and indecision which had
held him for weeks was no more. George knew
what he had to do.

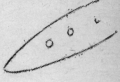

THIS
IS
WAR!

Boom!

Once...

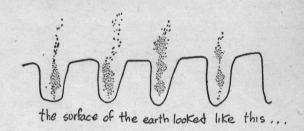

the surface of the earth looked like this . . .

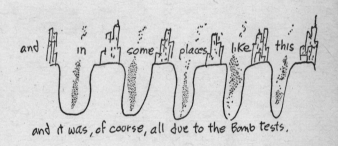

and it was, of course, all due to the Bomb tests.

Almost every country had its own Bomb.

If you've got a Bomb you're supposed to test it.

Like to see if it works.

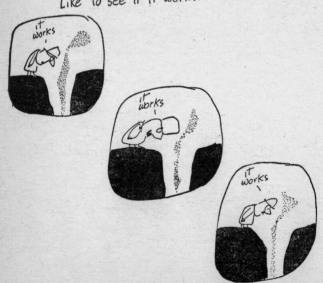

After each explosion the test areas were filled by government scientists who took readings and checked their instruments and issued a definitive statement.

Naturally the more tests there were the better the Bombs got to be.

But the skies began to grow darker

and people noticed it and said

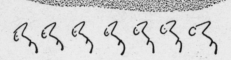
" I GUESS THE GOVERNMENT MUST HAVE ITS SOUND REASONS"

and went about their business.

Of course there was more going on than just Bomb tests.
For instance, as soon as one country discovered a bigger Bomb than its neighbor the first thing it did was call a disarmament conference.

HA!

sigh

and make a proposal -

and all the other countries replied:

"WE AGREE. JUST AS SOON AS WE CATCH UP."

So there was a dead lock

and people heard the news and said:

"THATS THE WAY THE BALL BOUNCES"   or   "THATS THE WAY THE COOKIE CRUMBLES."

and went about their business.

But the conferences continued.

while more and more countries developed their own Bomb. And naturally all of them had to be invited.

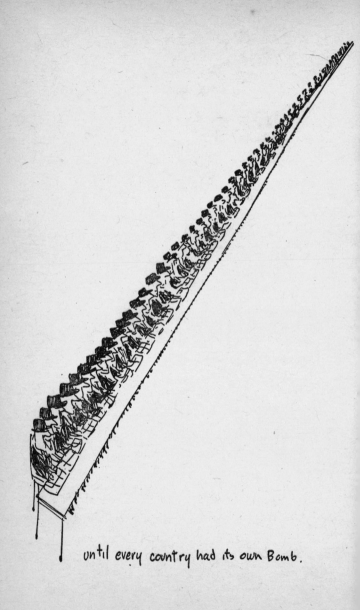

until every country had its own Bomb.

and even some towns..

and
even:

and people heard the news and said:

"THATS THE WAY THE ONION PEELS."

and went about their business.

Each test, no matter how small, was carefully checked for after effects. "THIS TEST HAS ADDED NO APPRECIABLE AMOUNT OF RADIO ACTIVE FALLOUT TO THE ATMOSPHERE."

But now the skies began to look like this.

and people noticed it and said:

"OF COURSE I'M CONCERNED BUT
WHAT CAN ONE PERSON DO?"

and went about their business.

The government began to get worried

"PEOPLE MAY GET TO THINK THOSE BIG BLACK FLOATING SPECKS ARE HARMFUL."

"WE MUST REASSURE THEM."

So they hired a public relations outfit...

BIG BLACK FLOATING SPECKS ARE VERY PRETTY!

BIG BLACK FLOATING SPECKS ARE GOOD FOR YOU!

which put on a big campaign.

But the campaign had no effect. People got more and more concerned.

Then the public relations outfit changed its tactics.

The public responded sympathetically. "WE'RE ON THE RIGHT TRACK AT LAST" said the public relations outfit.

Industry thrived.

World economy boomed.

The problem of over-
population seemed
somehow to diminish.

With the thickening of the specks, new businesses
were born. The world grew rich. Education prospered.
Art flourished.

It was
a new
renaissance

But soon countries grew fat and complacent. Bomb
production dropped off. And then — one day —
the black specks began to disappear.

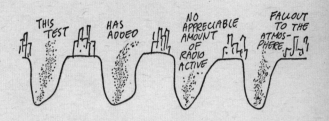

THIS TEST HAS ADDED NO APPRECIABLE AMOUNT OF RADIO ACTIVE FALLOUT TO THE ATMOSPHERE

So while half the people in the world worked on new improved Bombs—

SECRET

the other half worked on salves, medication, and storm windows.

And people saw the situation and said:

"THATS THE WAY THE SPEARMINT CHEWS"-

and went about their business.

Then one day...

"GENTLEMEN, I MAY BE TALKING OFF THE TOP OF MY HEAD - BUT I THINK I'VE DREAMED UP A BOMB THAT WILL BLOW UP THE WHOLE WORKS!"

"WHAT A DETERRENT FOR PEACE" said men on the inside.

But propagandists in other countries planted seeds of doubt.

NON-SENSE!

BALONEY

BLUFF!

So the men on the inside got together -

"THIS DETERRENT WILL NEVER BE EFFECTIVE UNTIL WE TEST IT!"

But nobody wanted to take the blame. "HEY!" said somebody, "WHY DON'T WE TAKE THE QUESTION TO THE PEOPLE!"

So it was decided. A referendum was announced.

STAND BEHIND YOUR GOVERNMENT. IT KNOWS WHATS BEST!

Men on the inside campaigned vigorously.

THIS TEST WILL ADD NO APARECIABLE AMOUNT OF RADIOACTIVE FALLOUT TO THE ATMOSPHERE.

The test was given an overwhelming mandate. the people said:

"NOW IS NO TIME TO SHOW LACK OF UNITY"

and they went about their business.

So they had the test.

and it worked.